THE GREAT COURT, TRINITY COLLEGE

CAMBRIDGE

Described by NOEL BARWELL
Pictured by E. W. HASLEHUST

BLACKIE & SON LIMITED
LONDON AND GLASGOW

BLACKIE & SON LIMITED
50 Old Bailey, London
17 Stanhope Street, Glasgow

BLACKIE & SON (INDIA) LIMITED
Warwick House, Fort Street, Bombay

BLACKIE & SON (CANADA) LIMITED
Toronto

Printed in Great Britain by Blackie & Son, Ltd., Glasgow

LIST OF ILLUSTRATIONS

BYRON'S POOL

CAMBRIDGE

To the sympathetic beholder one of the most potent charms of England lies in the singular diversity of its landscape. To him each district makes its special, its peculiar appeal. He is sensible everywhere of a real, if intangible, *genius loci*; and he is prone to seek the effect of some such spirit as well in the history of communities and bodies politic as in the lives of individuals. For him, then, there must needs be something of truth in the idea that much of the destinies of Oxford and Cambridge lay written upon the land at their gates. From the hills above Oxford a man may see the whole city at his feet. Generations of men have so seen it, and have so regarded it, subjectively—as a whole. At sundown, when the varied shape of tower and dome merge in a common outline, this impression of unity becomes unforgetably intensified; and but few, probably, of those who have found there the place of their education, will have left it without a sense of having shared in some common purpose. It has ever seemed the aim of Oxford to foster uniformity; of Cambridge, however unconsciously, to encourage the opposite in thought and manners. The sympathies which unite men of a Cambridge education are not therefore less strong, but they are subtler and less capable of expression in a phrase.

Cambridge is no city of spires. She lies belted with woods in the midst of a wide plain. To south, to west, to east stretches a lowland landscape, delicately moulded, rich in pasture and corn-bearing fields. Northwards a man need ride but a few miles across the fens to hear the bells of Ely, or at twilight to see the lantern of that ancient church preserve its solitary vision of the sun. Through this broad tract of country, whose every detail is typical of all which is most beautiful in the Eastern Midlands, winds that gentlest of English rivers, the Cam. Above Cambridge, it still bears its ancient name of Granta; at Ely it is the Ouse. The scenery along its upper reaches, though small in scale, is of singular merit to eyes which are not weary of "Nature's old felicities". Near Grantchester, a lock now marks an ancient bifurcation of the river, and here the stream widens to form a deep sequestered pool, shaded by a veritable arena of tall trees. Poet as well as peasant must often have bathed here and have made it a place of meditation. It was a favourite spot with Byron, and it is still called after him.

Passing from the countryside to within the boundaries of the University itself, nothing, perhaps, will seem more remarkable to the curious observer than the absence of that hard-featured grandeur with which the architecture of the Middle Ages was so deeply impressed. Cambridge goes back eight centuries; but there remains little to remind us of those many vicissitudes of mediæval life from which neither of the Universities emerged unscathed; for with the disappearance of Feudalism, the advent of the New Learning, and the breakdown of Monasticism, Cambridge assumed a richer dress, and the fine apparel of those days becomes her still. From that string of Tudor palaces whose broad lawns and well-nurtured gardens mark the lazy passage of the Cam, to those more distant Colleges of Jesus and Emmanuel, a grave tranquillity pervades the whole. This sense of peace and of contentment, so precious to the individual mind, seems largely due to that gracious domesticity which the Tudor architect so well knew how to impart even to the meanest of his college buildings. But to those later architects who practised here, while architecture was still an art in England, is owing that conscious, studied stateliness we now prize. The genius of Wren, which at Oxford in his tower of Christ Church with inimitable propriety seized upon and revivified for his purpose the Gothic style of architecture, as easily and as properly adapted itself to the more reticent temper of this University. The examples of his skill which may be seen at Pembroke and Emmanuel; the bridge at St. John's, built by his pupil Hawksmoor apparently from his designs; above all his great Library at Trinity, remain to show with what appreciation he met the contemplative character of the Cambridge mind, with what zest he lent his art to the commemoration of her material prosperity.

The first important period of building in Cambridge was the fourteenth century. Seven colleges were founded and provided with decent accommodation between 1324 and 1352. In the next century four more colleges were set up. While in the sixteenth century, from 1505 to 1595, another seven colleges were added to the University. Two other colleges have since arisen in Cambridge—Downing, built in 1805; and Selwyn, set up originally as a hostel in 1882, but now recognized as a "House" in all but the official sense of that expression. There are also two large and important colleges which are devoted to the higher education of women. Girton College, founded in 1867, is the oldest institution of its kind. Newnham College dates from 1871. That Cambridge should have been the first university in England to admit women to her studies and to her examinations is no more than fitting, when it is remembered that some six of her principal colleges were founded or endowed by great ladies. Members of Clare, Pembroke, Queens', Christ's, St. John's, and Sidney Sussex Colleges may, for this reason, very properly feel a certain debt to the sex.

Still more remarkable is the extent of royal benefaction in Cambridge. In Oxford only one College, Queen's, owes its existence directly to the patronage of royalty. At Cambridge there are five houses which can lay claim to the style of a royal foundation: King's, Trinity, Queens', Christ's, St. John's; and of these the first two were founded and endowed by reigning sovereigns. King's Hall—afterwards merged in Trinity—was planned by Edward II and endowed by Edward III; King's College was founded by Henry VI; and Trinity by Henry VIII, who further endowed several professorships in the University; Queen Margaret of Anjou and Elizabeth Woodville, Queen to Edward IV, are co-founders of Queens'; Lady Margaret Tudor was the foundress of Christ's and St. John's Colleges. But the patronage of England's monarchs did not end with the sixteenth century. Mary was a benefactor to Trinity. Queen Elizabeth attached Westminster School to that college by certain scholarships, and sent timber to and completed the chapel there. She also sent building material to Corpus Christi College. James I was always coming to Cambridge; but, like most of the Stuarts, did little for the University, unless a copy of his literary "works" be considered a benefaction. George I purchased the library of Bishop Moore of Ely and gave it to the University. He also founded the regius professorship of Modern History there; while George IV contributed to the building of what is now called the New Court at Trinity College. His brother, the Duke of Gloucester, was the first member of an English Royal family to be educated within the precincts of a university. He was of Trinity, where two portraits of him now hang. The House of Hanover has ever shown favour to Cambridge. Prince Albert, Consort to Queen Victoria, was its Chancellor, and his late Majesty King Edward VII, having himself spent a year at each of the Universities, sent his elder son, the late lamented Duke of Clarence, to Cambridge, where he was entered at Trinity and by his father's special command "kept" in college, attended the usual lectures, and lived the ordinary life of an undergraduate nobleman. The latest member

of the Royal family to enter the University is Prince
Leopold of Battenberg, whose period of residence at
Magdalene College has only recently terminated.

It seems never easy to explain to people un-
acquainted with English University life, the precise
difference between the University and the College.
The University, as a corporation teaching and grant-
ing degrees, is older than any college, and has its
own endowments. Now, however, that the colleges
have come and have established a social and do-
mestic tone which could not exist without them,
the University shows itself conscious of their value
in a great many ways. The Vice-chancellor is
elected from the number of Heads of Houses; the
Proctors are nominated by each college in rotation,
and the University expects and has now the power
to exact contributions from each college towards the
necessary expenses of the whole academy. Within
the colleges themselves there are three grades of
inmate: the Fellow, the Scholar, and the Pensioner.
The first must be of Bachelor standing at the time
of his election, and must shortly afterwards proceed
to a higher degree. He draws his stipend from the
endowments of the college. From this class are
drawn the college Tutors, Lecturers, and Deans, while
as many more "dons" devote their time to private
study. The scholars on the foundation draw their

stipends from the endowments of the college in accordance with the statutes or the terms of some special benefaction; while the term Pensioner comprises all those undergraduates who pay for everything they receive at college.

But the history of the English Universities must be considered as that of communities into whose lives colleges were introduced for a social rather than a scholastic purpose. Cambridge grew into a seat of learning during the latter half of the twelfth century, but the first College, Peterhouse, was not founded till 1284. Till then, the scholars who resorted to the place lodged where they could in the town. This was the practice at every university in Europe; and, even to-day, the Universities of Oxford, Cambridge, and Dublin afford the only exceptions to it.

Housed in dwellings mean enough to the eye and as certainly ungracious to the nose, the young scholars of those early days lived a life of what we should now call intolerable discomfort. Coarse vesture, scanty food, long hours in the "common schools", such were the dominant features in the student life of every youth who sought to acquire the book learning of his day. Nor did the foundation of the first few colleges sensibly alter these unhappy conditions. The aim of their founders was the removal by benefaction of some of the worst hardships to which the young scholar was

THE KITCHEN WALL, PETERHOUSE

then subjected. Thus provision was made for the bare necessaries of life—lodging, food, and raiment. Poverty was, of course, the first statutory qualification for membership. That the prosecution of certain studies was enjoined upon the beneficiaries, testifies less to a desire to further this or that branch of knowledge than to a not unnatural anxiety lest these young men should fall into idleness or other evil habits.

What was the town and what the university into which this new element of scholastic life now entered? Cambridge had a navigable river pouring its waters into the North Sea at the natural port of Lynn. Moreover, the town marked the junction of two Roman roads. It was a fertile spot; and its situation had struck the Conqueror as one of strategic importance. Here, therefore, he built a castle, the mound of which remains to this day. The structure itself was dismantled gradually during the fifteenth century. Some of the stone was used for the building of King's Hall, and some for King's College. "Hereby", writes Fuller in 1655, "that stately structure, anciently the ornament of Cambridge, is at this day reduced next to nothing." But during the twelfth and thirteenth centuries men might still look at that Norman keep and take heart of grace. Under its shadow had grown up a prosperous market town. On the one hand it was the greatest Fish Mart, on the other a town noted for one of the most important Fairs in the country. This Fair was held in a field hard by the village of Barnwell, that is to say, within two miles of the University town itself; it began on the feast of St. Bartholomew and lasted until the fourteenth day after the feast of the Exaltation of the Cross (Aug. 24—Sept. 14). It still survives as the principal pleasure show and Horse Fair of the shire.

With these advantages Cambridge, as a town, rose rapidly in importance. The Jews appeared in 1106; and during that and the succeeding century most of the religious orders had established themselves in the place. The Templars were the first to appear. They built their church sometime between 1120 and 1140. It is the earliest of the four round churches which have come down to us.

Our universities, like most other English institutions, were not made—they grew; and all we can say of the origin of Cambridge is, that before the thirteenth century was far advanced references to it as a "*studium generale*" or University creep into the state documents of the time. A migration from Oxford took place in 1209, and in 1231 a letter from King Henry III to the Mayor and bailiffs makes mention of a great influx of scholars "both from the regions near home and from beyond the seas". This document is also interesting as showing that the finding of lodgings

was a matter of no little difficulty to the scholars.
The King has to request the townspeople to deal
properly with the students in all such transactions.
When, therefore, Walter de Merton, the founder of
the College in Oxford which bears his name, bought
land at both Universities and endowed students in
those schools, his benefaction came none too soon.
His house and scholars at Cambridge are mentioned
in a document as early as 1259; and it was not till
1274 that he removed these scholars to the other
University. Ten years later was founded the first
exclusively Cambridge College. It was to consist of a
Master and fourteen Fellows, together with a number
of "bible clerks"—young men whose duty it was to
read to the Society at meal times. This College
was dedicated to St. Peter, and was known as "the
House of the scholars of St. Peter", or Peterhouse.
The founder was Hugh de Balsham, Bishop of Ely.

The reasons which dictated Merton's change of
policy can only be conjectured. To attempt to set
up a stable society in an obviously unstable community must have seemed to many a risky project.
A university was a body of students who possessed in
actual property little more than the gowns upon their
backs. At a word of plague or rapine they could, and
indeed did, migrate elsewhere. A college with buildings and land could not as easily or as profitably

take flight. From the point of view of a would-be benefactor, Cambridge, standing as it did "on the edge of the great wild"—to use Mr. J. W. Clark's words—might well seem to possess a less favourable situation than Oxford. It had, in the past, suffered a great deal from attack; and if the educationists of those days thought twice before running the risk of seeing their good works brought to nought in Cambridge, the subsequent history of the University very nearly bore out their worst fears; for the revolting peasants who followed the celebrated Wat Tyler entered Cambridge in considerable numbers, and, being joined by the great mass of the townsfolk, broke into Corpus Christi College. They burnt its archives, together with every other book and paper they could lay their hands on; and not content with this damage "done and committed", they repaired to St. Mary's and the Common Schools, where, seizing the University chests, they destroyed the muniments and made away with the funds.

Thus it is neither surprising if Merton should have felt doubtful of the continued prosperity of Cambridge, nor remarkable that twenty-eight years should have elapsed before Hugh de Balsham's venture in founding a college there should have met with the flattery of imitation. But the next college, that of Michael-house (merged afterwards, as was King's Hall, in

(C238)

THE OLD HALL, CORPUS CHRISTI COLLEGE

Henry VIII's great College of the Holy Trinity), was followed in quick succession by five other foundations:—Clare Hall, 1326; King's Hall, 1337; Pembroke Hall, 1347; Gunvil Hall (now Gonville and Caius College), 1348; Trinity Hall, 1350; and Corpus Christi College, 1352.

Perhaps a word concerning the nomenclature of Cambridge Colleges may fittingly find a place here. "College" is a late expression, as things go in Cambridge. The earliest words are *domus* and *aula*, respectively "house" and "hall": thus Peterhouse, Michaelhouse, and God's House (now Christ's College); and Clare Hall, Pembroke Hall, and Catharine Hall. This use of the word "hall" is ancient and honourable in Cambridge, and the fact that it has a different signification in Oxford, where it is used to denote a licensed lodging-house under a Master of Arts, should never have operated to prevent its retention in our University to-day. "The Hall of the Holy Trinity of Norwich" is perhaps forced by circumstance to preserve its ancient name; but when it calls itself "*The* Hall", it does so, one must hope, rather as a protest than in pride of singularity. Some popular errors or misapprehensions may here be noted under this head. The college styled in the Cambridge Calendar "Gonville and Caius" was originally founded by one Edmund Gonville, who pronounced his name "Gunvil". It was

later re-endowed and much enlarged by the celebrated Dr. Keys, who, conformable to the fashion
of his day, latinized his name for literary purposes
into "Caius". The latinized form of the one and
the more correct spelling of the other founder are
now used in writing down the name of the College;
but, colloquially, traditional usage still preserves the
English names in the pronunciation of their time.
The members of Queens' College, in virtue of two royal
foundresses, write the apostrophe after the final "s";
while Magdalene men insist on preserving the final
"e" in the name of their patron saint. Perhaps,
however, the most curious example of a wrong
name clinging to a House is presented by Jesus
College. This, the popular appellation, is no better
than a nickname. The college is not dedicated to
Our Saviour, but to "The Blessed Virgin Mary, St.
John the Evangelist, and the Glorious Virgin St.
Rhadigund". It happens to stand in the now obli-
terated and forgotten parish of Jesus; but this nickname from a past age continues to serve its old and
useful purpose. Another example is that of Pembroke College, founded by Marie, widow of Aylmer
de Valence, Earl of Pembroke. The foundress wished
her college to be styled "The Hall of Valence Marie",
and such is its proper name. Lastly, King's College
was dedicated to St. Mary and St. Nicholas.

Before turning to the more modern aspect of Cambridge, the subject demands that something should be said of those notable periods of prosperity, the fifteenth and sixteenth centuries. The evidence of the growth and power of the University during those years lies, for the visitor, in the number and magnificence of the buildings then undertaken which have survived till our own day the dual tests of time and taste. Of the original buildings of those early colleges to which reference has already been made next to nothing remains. The shell of the old court at Corpus is still standing; but this part of the college has been re-roofed, most of the windows in it are of a late period, and it is almost wholly covered with ivy. Some of the masonry forming the south wall of the Peterhouse kitchen is perhaps as old as anything in Cambridge; and this quaint corner of the oldest college is the subject of an illustration to the present volume. The Chapel of this college is of the seventeenth century. The Library is late Tudor. The Hall and Combination Room are part restorations and part a matter of fresh designing. The work was undertaken between 1866–70. Gilbert Scott, William Morris, Burne-Jones, and Ford Madox Brown had each a hand in it. Trinity Hall has been almost entirely rebuilt. All save the Library, which is late Tudor and which lies beyond the main quadrangle, is of late eighteenth-century design. The lodge and certain newer buildings are said to be commodious. They are none the less ugly. The rebuilding of Clare Hall began during the reign of Charles I and was continued during the inter-regnum; but it was not finished until the eighteenth century had entered upon the last quarter of its course. As it stands to-day, it is perhaps the most perfect example of the Carolian style in England. The little bow window over the gateway is remembered as the favourite seat of a certain fellow of the College, who lived and died more than a hundred years ago, and of whom it is recorded that, being at feud with the Master of his College, he chose this particular set of chambers, because of the chance it afforded him of successfully spitting at that unlucky dignitary as he entered or left the college precincts.

Pembroke College possessed till quite recently a really beautiful example of a fourteenth-century Dining-hall. The late Mr. Waterhouse alarmed the society by reporting it to be in danger of falling about their ears. He was commissioned, therefore, to take it down and to build them another. In executing the first part of these instructions he was observed to have recourse to dynamite. Less drastic methods might avail to remove the building which now occupies the place of that fine old Hall. In

ERASMUS' TOWER, QUEENS' COLLEGE

speaking of it the present writer is tempted to borrow the words of the learned Provost of King's in noticing the Library building by the same hand: "It could only suffer", says Dr. James, "by any description of it that I might write". Gonville Hall was another college destined to undergo a complete remodelling. Fortunately the rebuilding took place in the sixteenth century, and much of the work then undertaken remains to this day. It marked the munificence of its re-founder, and devoted master, the celebrated Dr. Caius. This extraordinary man was born in Norwich in 1510. He was of Gonville Hall, and, after taking the usual degrees, proceeded Doctor at Padua, where he lectured in Greek. His learning was prodigious and his reputation European. He lived to translate some Erasmus into English, to write numerous treatises of his own, to preside over the College of Physicians, to carry out various antiquarian researches, and to serve with distinction as Physician to Edward VI, Mary, and Elizabeth. He ended his days Master of his beloved College in Cambridge, where he lies buried. In his last illness he endeavoured to sustain life by a return to the natural nourishment of infancy; and divers dames of the town were privileged to minister to his wants in this respect. Being observed to be now "froward, peevish, and full of frets", and now tractable, docile, and of an amiable countenance, his moods and tempers were considered to vary with the individual source of his curious refreshment. Gonville and Caius College, as it is now called, possessed till recently three gateways of the time of Caius. That leading on to the street was inscribed the Gate of Humility; that between the first and second court, the Gate of Virtue; and the last, as leading to the hall where degrees were conferred, the Gate of Honour. Of these gates the two last mentioned have fortunately survived; but the first has given place to a large block of buildings designed by the late Mr. Waterhouse in his best Provincial Assurance manner. The visitor will be startled to read the words *Porta Humilitatis* above the doorway of this amazing pile.

The fifteenth century saw four more Colleges added to the list of Cambridge Houses: King's, 1441; Queens', 1448; St. Catharine's, 1473; Jesus, 1495. The first of these was designed to eclipse every other collegiate foundation in England. As finally settled by the will of Henry VI, its founder, the society consisted of seventy souls under the headship of a Provost. It is bound by sisterly ties to King Henry's other foundation, the College of St. Mary at Eton. Eton, indeed, was and is to King's College what Winchester has been to New College in Oxford. Till 1857 the scholars of Eton proceeded by right to scholarships and fellowships at King's. None but Etonians could come upon the foundation, and Kingsmen enjoyed the further privilege of proceeding to their degrees without any University examination. The Society ceded these privileges in the year named, and by its present statutes consists of a Provost, forty-six Fellows, forty-eight Scholars, of whom twenty-four hold "close" scholarships attached to Eton, two Chaplains, an Organist, and a Master of the Boys. The choristers on the foundation are required to be of gentle birth, and they have their education in an admirably equipped school under the special government of the College. Of the buildings which the founder not only contemplated but specified in a document drawn up by himself, nothing but the Chapel was so much as set out. The Gatehouse, the great Quadrangle, the Hall and Butteries, the Library, the Provost's Lodging, the Cloister with its garth, the Bell Tower, and the bridge across the river were planned and specified, but never undertaken on the lines which the founder so carefully laid down. The King died before he could sufficiently endow his college. His immediate successors in the Crown of England, to whom in language unforgetably solemn he commended the care of his foundation, did something for it; but egotism being stronger than piety in princes, those royalties of a later age who cared to patronize learning preferred to initiate rather than complete. The Chapel of King's College, however, owes a great deal to the munificence of the Sovereigns of England. It took more than a century in building, and cost for the stonework alone about £160,000, according to the present value of money. To the completion of this magnificent structure Edward IV, Richard III, Henry VII, Henry VIII, and Queen Elizabeth subscribed on a liberal scale. The window glass and the woodwork belong wholly to the sixteenth century, with here and there additions of a later date. The roof, had it been carried out by the first set of masons employed, would certainly have been "lierne" vaulted; but by the time the walls were ready to bear a roof at all, "fan" vaulting had come into vogue. The Chapel as it stands to-day presents without doubt one of the most beautiful interiors to be seen in England. The choir-screen and stalls are of Renaissance design, executed with a subtlety not to be matched on this side of the Alps. The Lectern is of the first quarter of the sixteenth century and is therefore nearly contemporaneous with the greater number of the stained-glass windows. In one of the side chapels is preserved an interesting specimen of a fifteenth-century pulpit, which on March 25 of every year, being the Annunciation of the Virgin, is brought forth into the church. From this pulpit a Fellow of the College preaches before the

University on the day named: a departure from the usual custom of meeting in Great St. Mary's which serves to mark the founder's wish that his college should occupy a pre-eminent place in Cambridge.

The sixteenth century saw the foundation and endowment of the two great colleges of Trinity and St. John's, the sister college to the latter, Christ's, and the rise of Magdalene, Emmanuel, and Sidney Sussex. Of these, St. John's was the first to attain eminence. Bishop Fisher, Cecil the great Lord Burleigh, and Archbishop Williams successively lent her their aid. She became *par excellence* an aristocratic college, and by the first decade of the nineteenth century could boast that she included among her *alumni* more men of note in the social and intellectual life of the country than any other college in either University could lay claim to. The first Court of this College has been much disturbed. The gateway is one of the finest examples of its period to be found anywhere; but, on entering the College, the eye is at once offended by a poor eighteenth-century range of buildings on the left, and a vast effort by the late Sir Gilbert Scott, by way of Chapel, on the right. The second Court, however, is well-nigh faultless. Here is late Tudor at its best; and in this small rosy-red brick of the period it finds the happiest material for the expression of its aims.

The further or third Court is Carolian. It is quaint and charming in its own rather odd fashion, and as seen from the river, whose waters here touch the very walls of its western range, contrives to bear a strangely impressive appearance. The Cam is here spanned by two bridges: one, a very beautiful example of Sir Christopher Wren's style—it was built by his pupil Hawksmoor—the other a Cockney Gothic affair commonly called "The Bridge of Sighs". This last connects the old Carolian building with a huge range built during the years 1827-31, which cost the college £78,000. Of the bridge itself, which is part of this dreadful building, it will be noticed that a certain decency of proportion — its one merit—renders it some degrees less detestable than the main structure to which it belongs.

Christ's College, the other "Lady Margaret" foundation, has undergone a great deal of rebuilding and not a few additions. The gateway from the street and most of the chambers to right and left of it are of the sixteenth century. The finest architectural possession of the college is its block of Fellows' buildings towards the garden. It would seem to be by a pupil of Inigo Jones, if not actually by the Master himself.

Magdalene is the only college in Cambridge which, in a sense, is of monkish origin. It was originally a cell of Croyland; and being endowed by Henry, second Duke of Buckingham, it soon came to be known as Buckingham College. In 1483 it is styled "Bokyngham College" and its inmates are described as "monachi". Lord Chancellor Audley, who changed the foundation into Magdalene College, refounded it for an ordinary academical society, after the house, as a cell of Croyland Abbey, had escheated to the Crown. This college does not elect its Master: the headship of the House being in the gift of the "owner of Audley End". At present, therefore, the Lords Braybrooke present to the Mastership. Magdalene is a picturesque and commodiously arranged college, and, though small, has many attractive features. The most interesting building is that erected in the seventeenth century, primarily with the idea of providing suitable accommodation for the library of Samuel Pepys the diarist. The latest addition, a range brought close to the riverside, is perhaps the most successful in design and colour of any of the more recent buildings in the University.

The College of the Holy and Undivided Trinity, though inheriting much from the earlier college—King's Hall—which was set up by Edward II and his son Edward III, owes almost everything to King Henry VIII. It was typical of this monarch that, after somewhat maltreating Wolsey's foundation at

Oxford and paying not too much attention to Henry VI's or King's College at Cambridge, he should have set about founding Trinity with the plain intent of eclipsing both. The College as we see it to-day, is the largest and wealthiest in either University. It is founded for a Master, sixty Fellows at the least, and eighty Scholars. In full term the resident members number nearly eight hundred souls. From the first, the buildings were set out to accommodate an unusually large society. The Great Court, with its Chapel, Gatehouse, Hall, Master's Lodge, and rows of chambers, broken here by a tower, there by a turret, occupies over two acres of ground. The character of its architecture is for the most part Tudor; for the restorations and alterations which have from time to time taken place have not been permitted to stray far from the traditional style of the Court. A further court—the Cloister or Neville's Court—consists of two ranges of Jacobean design, modified by later hands so as to fare better than they otherwise would beside Sir Christopher Wren's great Library building, which here occupies the entire western side of the quadrangle, even projecting above and beyond it on either side. In addition to these two spacious courts there are three other quadrangles, all of recent date. These are fortunately so situated that the sightseer can easily avoid looking at them.

GATEWAY, ST. JOHN'S COLLEGE

Emmanuel College possesses one court of the founder's time, and beautiful it is. It is rarely shown to the ordinary visitor, but those who care for simple unpretending work of this period (1584) have only to ask for the dovecot garden. The main Court of the College is of the seventeenth and eighteenth century. Wren made the design for the Chapel, which was built between 1668–78. The Court is finely proportioned and has always been admired.

Sidney Sussex College, the last college to belong to the sixteenth century, has been harshly dealt with. A charming Elizabethan college has been ruthlessly turned into a thoroughly bad stucco dwelling gothicized in the Wyatt manner. It has its treasures: a fine garden, good pictures, and some handsome plate.

We have now traced the main periods of Cambridge building. We have said very little of the life of the University or the growth of the town during these four hundred years. It is, indeed, hard to contemplate the visible memorials of those days without imagining a social life grander and happier for the individual man than could ever have been the case. Almost everything which makes for the amenities of college life as we see it to-day is comparatively speaking modern. To picture the life of scholars young and old even so late as the sixteenth century, we must be prepared to learn strange things. Fireplaces

were few and far between. Folk gathered as much
as possible in the Common Hall of the College. Here
was set a brazier of charcoal, its fumes poisonous and
disagreeable finding their way through a lantern or
louvre in the roof. Rushes were upon the floor, if
it were not tiled or paved. Windows having glass
in them were not common before the fifteenth century. The sanitary arrangements were primitive, ill-
managed, and consequently wretched. Street lighting
was unknown. Scholars slept two and often more
in a bed; and went, as did everyone else, naked to
their beds. The advantages of a bedfellow in those
bitter winters were obvious. It was equally obvious
that those who shared a chamber, and so often a bed,
should be well suited to one another; and parents
expressed a not unnatural anxiety on this head.
Letters exist in which the Tutor, who usually occupied a bed apart in a chamber for five persons, of
whom four would be his pupils, is asked to choose
carefully a bedfellow "gentle and virtuous" for the
youthful freshman. The average age of entering was
about fourteen during the earlier periods, but rose to
sixteen during the latter centuries of which we have
been writing. Most college offences were punishable
by whipping, graver imprudences meeting with public
chastisement executed by a menial in the Common
Hall of the College. Fellows of M.A. standing could

be put in the college "stocks", and often were so handled. The pedagogic notion that intellectual advancement is furthered by the application of physical pain was not confined to the grammar schools, and parents were often eager to place their sons under the care of a strong-armed college tutor. "Prey Grenefield", wrote a certain lady to a Cambridge Tutor in the time of Henry VI, "to send me faithfully worde ho Clemit Paston hathe do his dever i' lernyng, and if he hathe nought do well nor wyll nought amende, prey him that he wyll trewly belash him tyll he wyll amend, and so did ye last maystr and ye best en he had att Caumbreg." As time went on, however, the life of the ordinary pensioner became comfortable enough; but, unhappily, the scholar on the Foundation and the Sizar, or poorest of the juniors, one who paid for his education by the performance of menial offices, remained objects of contempt with the more wealthy undergraduates. Before the end of the fifteenth century, pensioners "in Fellows' Commons" had made their appearance in Cambridge. They were allowed to dine with the Fellows at the High Table, wore richly embroidered gowns and enjoyed many other privileges and distinctions. A higher order still was that of persons who entered as "Noblemen". Many of the latter class lived in College and "kept" there in some state. For example, in 1624 Lord Maltravers and his brother William Howard, sons of the then Earl of Arundel and Surrey, came up to St. John's College with a retinue of servants. It was requested that the brothers might occupy one room "with a pallett for the groome of their chamber"; while "the rest of his lordship's company, being two gentlemen, a groome of the stable, and a footman, might be lodged in the town near the College".

But the sixteenth and seventeenth centuries, for all the patronage of learning affected by prince and peer alike, were troublous times for the scholar. Much wit was needed to guide him through those political and religious conflicts which at times threatened to bring the University to dissolution. Doctors and Masters were for ever being ousted, driven overseas, or thrown into prison. No man knew when he might not be called upon to exchange a deanery for a dungeon. Let one example suffice. On the death of Edward VI, Lady Jane Grey was at once proclaimed Queen by order of Northumberland. On 16 July the Lady Mary was but five miles from Cambridge, at the house of Sir Robert Huddlestone. There she heard Mass and pushed on into Suffolk, where she met her supporters. The Duke of Northumberland with his army arrived in Cambridge five days later. He was Chancellor of the University

WREN'S BRIDGE, ST. JOHN'S COLLEGE

and a man zealous in promoting its prosperity. How far the residents believed in his cause we know not; but there seemed little apprehension of the fate which in reality awaited him. The Vice-Chancellor and many of the Heads supped with him that night, and on the morrow he set off for Bury. His return was speedy. And here in the Market-place, bereft of his former supporters, he was obliged, in the presence of the Mayor, Vice-Chancellor, and the rest of the Cambridge notables, to proclaim Mary Queen. He then repaired in some state to King's College, where, at a late hour that night, he was arrested by one Roger Slegge, the sergeant-at-arms, who was permitted to enter the gates unmolested, though, as Fuller says, "that College was fenced with more privileges than any other foundation in the University".

The Popish reaction burst out at Cambridge with almost incredible swiftness. On a certain day "Doctor Sandys, the Vice-Chancellor, on the ringing of the Schools' bell, went according to his custom and office, attended with the Bedells into the Regent House and sat down in the chair according to his place. In cometh one Master Mitch with a rabble of some twenty Papists, some endeavouring to pluck him from the chair, others the chair from him, all using railing words and violent actions. The Doctor, being a man of mettle, groped for his dagger and probably had despatched some of them had not Dr. Bill and Dr. Blyth by their prayers and entreaties persuaded him to patience." He was, in due course, despoiled, deprived, and cast into prison. But there were other losses which the University was called upon to suffer during these two hundred years: direct loss of treasure, and damage to those fair fabrics which the piety of benefactors had bestowed upon the community. Association of ideas is strong, and the Reformers were probably justified by circumstances in most of their destructive operations. Yet the finer spirits must have felt keenly the demolition of many objects irreplaceable by the hand of man. Good Dr. Caius kept what he dared of Mass books, vestments, and antique church ornaments, and seems to have hidden them away; but they were discovered and destroyed; and probably nothing but the degree of eminence to which he had then attained as a physician saved him from sharing the fate of his treasures. As for the Puritans under Cromwell, they did less damage than they might have done. King's College Chapel, the glory of the University, they wholly spared; and the various Colleges were called upon for less tribute than the experiences of other corporations and the rough usage of those times might have prepared their inhabitants to expect.

During the early part of the reign of Charles I

"the University", says Fuller, "began to be much beautified in buildings, every College either shedding its skin with the snake, or renewing its bill with the eagle, having their courts or at leastwise their fronts and gatehouses repaired and adorned. But the greatest alterations were in their chapels, most of them being graced with the accession of organs." Many of the chapel ornaments were subsequently defaced by Cromwell; but, as has already been stated, King's was left untouched in the matter of its fabric, its glass, and its brasses. The elaborate tombs in Caius Chapel were not injured; and the much earlier tomb—that of Hugh Ashton—in St. John's was also left undisturbed. The Fellows of Peterhouse took the precaution to bury the glass which filled the east window of their chapel. It lay undiscovered, and all of it has now been replaced. Certainly Cromwell got some plate out of the University, but this tribute was as nothing when compared to that which went to Charles. Trinity sent practically its all. King's, as the earlier Royal Foundation, could not afford to be behindhand. St. John's was Tory almost to a man, and away went most of her finest silver. "Her contribution", says the present Master, "was £150 in money and 2065 ounces, grocer's weight, of silver plate." Among the pieces so lost were some bearing the names of Thomas Wentworth, Lord

Strafford, and of Thomas Fairfax. For this the College later suffered much indignity. Cromwell surrounded the place, took the Master a prisoner, and "confiscated the communion plate and other valuables". Nearly every College had paid tribute; but the fact that Cambridge was providentially spared the duty of nursing, either then or afterwards, any part of a Stuart Court, enabled her to save for posterity as much in gold and silver works of handicraft as Oxford lost. Thus the Cambridge plate as it stands to-day is the finest collection of its kind in existence.

Throughout these two hundred years—years of Renaissance, of Reformation, of Revival, of Revolution—Cambridge poured forth an unending stream of men destined for the highest places in church, in state, in scholarship, and in letters. Coverdale, Fox, Ridley, Latimer, Cranmer, Gardiner, Parker, Grindal, Whitgift, Bancroft, Andrews, Cosin, Williams, Taylor, Stillingfleet, Sancroft, Tillotson, Tenison are her divines; and of the seven "nonjuring" bishops, five, including the Primate, were Cambridge men. The Protector Somerset, Cecil the great Lord Burleigh, his kinsman of Salisbury, Walsingham, Essex, Fulke Greville, Sir John Harrington, Chief Justice Coke, Sir Nicholas Bacon and his son Francis, Lord Verulam (commonly but wrongly styled Lord Bacon), Sir William Temple, Oliver Cromwell are figures

FISHER LANE AND GREAT BRIDGE

which are painted large upon the canvas of history; and in a dark corner are inscribed the names, at once famous and infamous, of Judge Jeffreys and Titus Oates. The lists of Cambridge scholars, poets, and prose writers of this age is no less remarkable. Roger Ascham, Sir John Cheke, Sir Thomas Smith, Jeremy Taylor, Thomas Fuller; the poets Spenser, Harvey, Marlowe, Greene, Fletcher, Ben Jonson, Heywood, Andrew Marvell, Milton, Cowley, Donne, Dryden, Herbert, Herrick, are names likely to live so long as the English language be spoken. Among Cambridge antiquaries we find the names of Stowe, Leland, and Strype. In medicine Cambridge was the foremost English school, and the names of Caius, Butler, Gilbert, and Harvey have a permanent place in the history of that Faculty. Three celebrated men of letters—Shirley, Lodge, and Lilley—migrated from Oxford to Cambridge. Wolsey, when he founded in Oxford his Cardinal's College — now styled Christ Church —came to King's College and King's Hall in Cambridge for many of his first Fellows. A Cambridge College, Pembroke, gave no fewer than four Heads to Oxford Houses during the latter half of the sixteenth century; and of this same College was Bishop Fox, the founder of Corpus Christi College in Oxford, and of two professorships there. In the New World, with the names of "the Pilgrim Fathers", are

remembered those of Hooker of Peterhouse, of Eliot
the "Indian Apostle" who took his degree in 1622,
and of John Harvard of Emmanuel, the founder of
America's oldest House of Learning. Horrocks and
Flamsteed, the astronomers, founded a Cambridge
School of Astronomy which has since taken the
foremost place in the development of that science.

The Cambridge of our own day contains much that
is reminiscent of those two hundred years. During the
sixteenth and seventeenth centuries academical dress
settled itself into the form in which for the most we
now see it. But something has come down to us
of even earlier days. Cambridge is not unjustly
proud of the fact that, unlike Oxford, the shape of its
hood has remained practically unaltered since the
fourteenth century. A notable mediæval garment still
worn at Cambridge, and not elsewhere to be found,
is the *Cappa Clausa* or "closed cope", used by the
Vice-Chancellor and by certain Doctors of Divinity,
Law, and Physic on special occasions. It is of scarlet
cloth with an ermine hood and trimmings. It must
not be confused with the scarlet gowns worn by all
doctors in the several Faculties on gala days. Over
the gate of Queens' College the curious may see a
rude representation of a doctor so robed; but a really
fine example of this dress as worn in the sixteenth
century may be seen on the brass to the memory of

John Argentein, D.D., M.D. (1507), in King's College Chapel. It was during the sixteenth century that the present style of M.A. gown and that of the Law gowns worn at Cambridge by Doctors of Laws and in the Courts by King's Counsel came into use. The style is fundamentally that of the ordinary walking dress of a notable of the end of the fifteenth century. A robe of this kind, as an over-garment, obtained all over Europe during the succeeding hundred years, and it would appear to have been Italian in origin. An example of the academical form of this garment may be seen on a brass at Croxton in Cambridge-shire, where is represented the figure of one Edward Leeds, LL.D., a Master of Clare Hall, who died in 1589. The strings now worn on all Cambridge gowns would seem to have come into general use about this time. In early times gowns were "closed" garments, and were put on over the head; and after it became lawful to wear them open in front, strings were used to tie the gown across the breast, and they were so worn until quite recently. Three other survivals of the costume of this later period may be noted. They are all peculiar to Cambridge. For example, the Proctor assumes on certain occasions an upper garment called a "ruff". Over this he wears his hood in the ordinary way. On certain other occasions, however, he must wear his hood "squared", that is, so folded that it presents the appearance of a large square cape. The method of arranging this dress has been handed down, as has a pattern "ruff", from Proctor to Proctor; but nowadays the repositories of such traditions are more often the Proctors' men, who, in these matters, perform the offices which judges expect of their clerks. The full dress of a Proctor's man—or "bull dog", as he is vulgarly called—is picturesque enough, for it is of a seventeenth-century pattern and consists in a long blue cloak studded with brass buttons. With this he carries a halberd. The Chancellor or Vice-Chancellor in procession is always preceded by two graduates, of M.A. standing at least, who are styled Esquire Bedells. The maces which these gentlemen carry on such occasions were given by George Villiers, Duke of Buckingham, the favourite of James I. The Duke was elected Chancellor of the University by the narrow majority of five votes. Another old custom, full of associations for Cambridge men, is the ringing of Curfew at Great St. Mary's Church. The University bell rings the Curfew nightly from nine of the clock till ten minutes past the hour. The date of the month is also struck by one of the same peal of bells. More curious, however, is the fact that the service, or, more properly speaking, the "office" of Compline, is commemorated at Trinity

Hall by the ringing of a bell there nightly at ten o'clock.

Many echoes of those "Disputations" which in mediæval times took the place of examinations may be followed in the Cambridge of to-day. The office of "Moderator" is with us still; Junior and Senior "Sophisters" are those who are on the road to becoming "Questionists"; and "Wranglers" are those who issue with honours from the supposed contest. A person qualifying for a medical degree when reading or submitting his finished "Thesis" is said to "Keep an Act" (i.e. a Disputation) for that degree. The origin of the word Tripos is not yet settled. Perhaps it derived itself from some sort of stool. Anyhow, by the middle of the eighteenth century, the Tripos had come to mean a sheet of paper upon one side of which were printed the names of those who had attained Honours in the Mathematical School, whilst upon the other was a copy of Latin Verses. Sheets of this Tripos paper were thrown by the Moderators from the gallery of the Senate House into the crowd assembled below. But until this same century was some way advanced another set of verses, usually very scurrilous in character, were recited by a sort of University Buffoon, who came also to be called "The Tripos". Licensed revellers were well-known institutions in both Universities throughout the Middle Age; but it was not until this Tripos fellow had been the subject of many scandals, protests, and warnings, that he was finally abolished.

The history of the English Universities in the eighteenth century has yet to be written; and though much material for such a history is accessible to the humblest enquirer, it is not possible in so short an essay as the present to do more than touch—and that very lightly—upon the salient features of Cambridge life during this, perhaps the most diverting period of the University's existence.

It is still fashionable to believe the Church and both the Universities to have passed the whole of these hundred years in a species of post-prandial slumber. Colleges are said to have become mere port-drinking societies; and the daily life of the Cathedral Chapters has been described quite as tersely and as disobligingly by numerous writers. Truly, the manners of the time were not over nice; but the impartial student of morals can well trace throughout the century a steady, if slow, revival from that dire sort of profligacy which marked the social life of the Stuart period. For the first time since the age of the Tudors, English architecture and the other arts not only revived, but attained the dignity of a conscious and coherent style. Gainsborough, Romney, Reynolds took the place once filled by such as Lely.

Wren, Hawksmoor, Vanbrugh, Adam gave to many an English building a fame which has not been confined to these islands. An intelligent taste in furniture, plate, porcelain, and fabrics became almost general in decent society. Music was widely cultivated, and literary effusions which did not conform, however dully, to the accepted models of the day found neither publisher nor reader.

Every merit and, it must be admitted, every demerit of the age is observable in the life of the University during these hundred years. Certainly there was a prodigious decay in University ceremonial, and the antiquaries shook their heads not perhaps without reason. Poor Hearne, noting the first Shrove-Tuesday morning on which the ancient "Pancake bell" did not ring in Oxford, ventured upon the aphorism: "When laudable old customs alter, 'tis a sign learning dwindles". Baker, Cole, and Gunning at Cambridge were doomed to see many cherished quaintnesses pass from the daily life of the academy. The ceremonies attending the Creation of Doctors in the several Faculties were gradually shorn of their symbolic splendour. These had involved in each case the use of a Ring and a Book. A candidate for a Doctorate in Law might be seen at such times to engage in a whispered colloquy with the Professor of his Faculty. This, perhaps the most picturesque

and most formal part of the ceremony of Creation, was known as "solving a question in the ear
of the Professor". Good Master Gunning could not
have failed to take pleasure in the circumstances
which attended the University Sermon on Tuesday
in Holy-week. On this day the sermon was preached,
not in Great St. Mary's, but in the Anglo-Saxon
Church of St. Benet. Before the sermon the preacher
was directed to say: "John Meer, Esquire Bedell, long
since of this University, gave a tenement situate in
this parish; in consideration whereof the sermon is
here this day. He left a small remembrance to the
officers of this University provided they were present
at the Commemoration; and was also not unmindful
of the poor in the Tolbooth and Spittal-house." At
the conclusion of the sermon a distribution was made
of this "small remembrance". It worked out at three
shillings and fourpence for the preacher, sixpence
for the Vice-Chancellor, and fourpence each for the
other dignitaries. A disbursement of three shillings
covered the other part of this amiable bequest!

During the whole of this period the University exer-
cised its ancient right of supervising all weights and
measures. Officers known as Taxors performed the
necessary testing, and at such times were authorized
to destroy any faulty measures which came under
their observation. There existed, too, for the pun-

THE MARKET PLACE

ishment of disorderly women, a University prison or bridewell called "the Spinning House", and one of the duties of the Proctors consisted in the visitation and inspection of any quarter of the town or its immediate environs in which vice was reputed to lurk. The Spinning House existed, as a building, within the recollection of the writer. It stood on ground now occupied by the Fire Station in Regent Street. These particular jurisdictions and the fact that the Vice-Chancellor took precedence of the Mayor at all public functions constituted the chief ground for that ill feeling between Town and Gown which was a notorious feature of Cambridge life even as late as 1850. The eighteenth century in Cambridge actually opened with a singularly unseemly fracas between the Municipal and University authorities. The Mayor himself and two of the Aldermen were implicated. The circumstances may be gathered from the "humble submission" of the former, dated October 2, 1705, in which he pleads guilty to having "denied unto Sir John Ellys, the Vice-Chancellor, the precedence in the joynt seat at the upper end of the guildhall . . . which refusal was the occasion of a great deal of contempt and indignity offered by some rude persons to the said Vice-Chancellor and his attendants". The "submission" of Mr. Francis Perry and his colleague followed in due course. These gentlemen owned to having opposed the Vice-Chancellor, "whereby divers unworthy affronts and indignities were occasioned the said Vice-Chancellor". Their submission did not come for the asking. Till they were made, however, the University authorities had "discommuned" half the townsfolk: which meant that an undergraduate who dared to deal with the burgesses might be sent down, whilst a graduate, for the same conduct, might be deprived of his degrees. This jurisdiction is still retained.

During this century sport became a prominent and important feature of University life. No longer confined, as were the students of an earlier day, to the precincts of the University, nor fenced about with clerical rules aiming at an almost monkish propriety, graduates and undergraduates began to ride, hunt, and shoot over the countryside. Towards the close of the century the crowd of "persons of quality" who attached themselves to the University as Noblemen or Fellow Commoners necessarily included a number of "raffish" spirits, who cared little for the convenience of others. A satirical advertisement touching this question appeared in the *Cambridge Chronicle* for 30 August, 1787, in which the neighbouring farmers, after announcing that their corn is in many places still standing, "beg the favour of the Cambridge gunners, coursers, and poachers, whether gentlemen, barbers, or gyps of Colleges", to let them get home their crops; and they continue: "If we might breed on our own premises a bird or a hare for ourselves, and have a day's shooting for our landlords, or our own friends, we should acknowledge it a great indulgence and politeness!" But a good deal of miscellaneous sport could be had within actual hail of the Colleges. "In going over land now occupied by Downing Terrace," says Gunning, "you generally got five or six shot at snipe. Crossing the Leys you entered on Cow Fen. This abounded with snipes. Walking through the osier bed on the Trumpington side of the brook you frequently met with a partridge and now and then a pheasant." But, for the undergraduates and the juniors generally, there were amusements enough. Though expressly forbidden, cock-fighting was popular; and there were more gaming, taverning, and the like diversions than sober-minded persons could be expected to approve of. Not only the students, but the seniors fell into cliques or sets each with its favourite coffee-house, where one might peruse the news sheets, make a bet, or pick a quarrel. Clubs, for the most part of an avowedly convivial nature, sprang into being, some of which, like The True Blue, remain to this day.

With the seniors, horse-exercise and bowls were popular pastimes. The Cambridge bowling greens were, and are, justly celebrated; and agreeable riding was to be had in most directions out of Cambridge. Along "The Backs" the mounting stones put up at this time may still be seen. Those Fellows of Colleges who held livings or curacies just outside the town rode to and from their cures in the performance of their duties. Other folk, like Dr. Samuel Peck, rode daily to the town on matters of private business. It is recorded of this worthy member of Trinity College that he gave advice on legal subjects for nothing. "Sam Peck never takes a fee," he would say. But he was wont to add that he saw no objection to a "present" in return for his services. Thus presents — mostly in kind — invariably followed upon any disbursement of his legal knowledge. The figure of Sam Peck, mounted on his horse and loaded with gifts, is preserved for us in a print now somewhat scarce, but of which a copy hangs in the smaller Combination Room at Trinity. This charming picture is also interesting as showing that for a celibate Fellow of a College in those days the present of a pair of lady's stays was not thought wholly unsuitable. Fellows of Colleges, it should be borne in mind, were by statute debarred from matrimony; and, saving the case of some few Civilians, i.e. graduates in Civil Law, they were bound to take Holy Orders. Thus were the Universities filled with numbers of gentlemen who

LIBRARY STAIRCASE, ST. JOHN'S COLLEGE

in order to teach pagan literature on a comfortable
stipend, had been forced to assume the garb and too
often the duties of the Christian priesthood. To give
them their due, however, they met the statutable re-
quirements of the place with a fortitude which never
sought to escape the gibes of those professed cynics
in which the age abounded; and there is surely a
healthy candour in the answer which a young Cambridge clergyman returned to Mr. Gunning's congratu-
lations on his appointment to a convenient living.
"My predecessor," said he, "was a man of my own
age, but was providentially attacked with gout in
the stomach, and died before he could receive medical attention."

The eighteenth century was pre-eminently an age
of oddities. Just as people collected books, china,
and rare prints, so in a sense they collected men,
and delighted to record whatever was whimsical in
their fellow creatures. The reminiscences of Henry
Gunning, sometime Esquire Bedell, teem with delight-
ful anecdotes. To students of men and manners,
it is one of the best books in the language. Its
comparative rarity must excuse the present writer for
drawing so largely upon it. Of Gunning's recollections
of the seniors of his young days none are better than
his stories of Dr. Samuel Ogden. Dr. Ogden took
his first degree as early as 1737, his D.D. in 1753,

and was appointed Professor of Geology in 1764. Visitors to the Round Church may like to hear of him, for there was he wont to preach. He was extremely fond of the pleasures of the table; and, while it is not expressly stated of him, there seems good cause to believe that like that fine old exciseman immortalized by Hawthorne in his preface to *The Scarlet Letter*, "there were flavours on his palate which had lingered there not less than sixty years". His was the saying: "A goose is a silly bird—too much for one and too little for two". At a dinner party, on a dish of ruffs and reeves coming up very much underdone, he answered his hostess's enquiry as to their merit by observing, "They are admirable, madam, *raw*! What must they have been had they been *roasted*?" When dining at Wimpole with Lord Hardwick, High Steward of the University, the butler, in mistake for champagne—then a great rarity—handed round glasses of pale brandy. Lord Hardwick himself instantly detected the error, but was too late to prevent Dr. Ogden emptying his glass. Lord Hardwick could not suppress an exclamation of surprise. "I did not mention it to you, my lord," said Ogden, "because I felt it my duty to take whatever you thought fit to offer me, if not with pleasure, at least in silence."

It is a true saying that "where there be strange folk there will be stranger doings", and the history of

Cambridge in the eighteenth century is charged with accounts of the oddest happenings. Could anything be more extraordinary, for example, than the circumstances which attended the election of Provost George at King's College in January, 1743? Twenty-two of the Fellows were for George, sixteen for Thackeray, and ten for Chapman, who was the Tory candidate. A regular faction fight ensued. The election was bound by statute to take place in the Chapel, and there the Fellows remained in conclave for thirty-one hours. Neither side would give way, and until they had agreed on their man none were permitted to stir out of the Chapel, "nor none permitted to enter", says a historian in 1753. An unsigned letter from Cambridge, quoted by Sir Henry Maxwell Lyte in his history of Eton College, gives a graphic account of these incidents: "The Fellows went into Chapel on Monday before noon in the morning as the statute directs. After prayer and sacraments they began to vote. . . . A friend of mine, a curious man, tells me he took a survey of his brothers at the hour of two in the morning, and that never was a curious or more diverting spectacle. Some, wrapped in blankets, erect in their stalls like mummies; others asleep on cushions like so many gothic tombs; here a red cap over a wig; there a face lost in the cape of a rug. One blowing a chafing-dish with a surpliced sleeve;

another warming a little negus or sipping 'Coke upon Littleton' i.e. tent and brandy. Thus did they combat the cold of that frosty night, which has not killed many of them to my infinite surprise." It is worth noting this determination of the Fellows of King's to act statutably, for the air was pretty full of unstatutable proceedings afterwards. It was apparently as a protest against some irregularity of this kind that one of the Scrutators (Mr. Tyrwhitt of Jesus) refused his key to the Vice-Chancellor when that dignitary desired to fix the University seal to a loyal address to the Crown on the subject of the American Rebellion. Dr. Farmer, however, was not a man to be baulked by trifles. He obtained the services of a blacksmith, and the seal was put to its appointed purpose without further delay.

Dr. Farmer was Master of Emmanuel, and one of the best known men of his time. With Malone, Reed, and Steevens he formed a coterie which was known in Cambridge as "the Shakespeare gang". Farmer knew the Elizabethans by heart, and he made Emmanuel Parlour, as the Combination Room of the College was then called, a centre of literary table-talk. His was an amiable personality. Though a strong Tory, he never allowed political bias to impair his friendships. "This is a Whig pipe, Master Gunning," he would say, with a sly twinkle. "It has a

FELLOWS' GARDEN AND POND, CHRIST'S COLLEGE

twist the wrong way." It was in Emmanuel Parlour that Dr. Johnson made one of his best sallies. The story is told by Isaac Reed, who was present. Someone asked why county squires should be addicted to rural sport above everything else. "Sir," said Dr. Johnson, "I have found out the reason of it, and the reason is that they feel the vacuity which is in them less when they are in motion than when they are at rest." It was during Dr. Farmer's mastership that Emmanuel celebrated the two hundredth anniversary of its foundation. For some days before the actual feast which was to take place in honour of the occasion, the inhabitants of the College were delighted with the spectacle of several "lively turtles" disporting themselves in tubs of water. William Pitt and the Earl of Euston, then the Members of Parliament for the University, were present at the banquet. The convivialities were kept up in the Parlour till a very late hour. Here Dr. Randall, the Professor of Music, "was called upon for his celebrated song in the character of a drunken man. The representation was so faithfully given that Mr. Pitt was completely deceived, and expressed some anxiety lest the worthy professor should meet with an accident when leaving the College."

But good Dr. Farmer was never more in his element than when sitting in what was called "the

Critics' Row" at the Playhouse specially set up during the weeks in which Stourbridge Fair held the attention of the three counties. Mention has already been made of this celebrated Fair. During the eighteenth century it was by far the largest Fair in the country. Every trade was represented, and here many of the good folk of Cambridgeshire, Huntingdon, and the Isle of Ely made the principal part of their household purchases for the year. People came from London and elsewhere to be present at the opening festivities. The declaration of the Fair was a matter of University as well as civic ceremonial. The Vice-Chancellor and the other University officers, attended by the noblemen and other notables, drove to the Fair, which was duly proclaimed by the Registrary of the University. The Senior Proctor provided cakes and wine at the Senate House before starting. To the University dignitaries and their guests was set apart a certain Tiled Booth, where they dined. The menu at the Vice-Chancellor's table never varied. It consisted of a large dish of herrings, a neck of pork roasted, a plum pudding, a leg of pork boiled, a pease pudding, a goose, and a huge apple pie, while a round of beef graced the centre of the board. Before the end of the century this dinner had degenerated into a sort of oyster luncheon. During this and the Midsummer or "Pot" Fair there was a deal of drunken and

riotous behaviour not confined, alas! to the townsfolk or the peasant classes. It is reported that tipsy
Masters of Arts, many Fellows of Colleges, and clergy-
men were to be seen with linked arms jostling the
passers-by.

To read but this side of University history one
might suppose an academy in which such things were
possible would hardly be able to claim to have done
much for learning during this period. But Cambridge
was no worse as a school for manners than was
any other place of education at this time; while the
period is one to which we look back to-day as the
age of Newton, Bentley, and Porson,—names which
alone are sufficient to raise the University into the
first place as a seat of learning. The poets, Prior,
Gray, Coleridge, and Wordsworth had their education in Cambridge before the century closed. So
also did Laurence Sterne. Halifax, the two Wal-
poles, Lord Camden, Lord Chesterfield, Lord Ellen-
borough, Lord Bathurst, Lord Thurloe, Pitt the
younger, Castlereagh, Wilberforce, Denman were
some of the illustrious Cambridge men who found
places in the great world of that day; while Paley
and Charles Simeon were prominent in the religious
life of the time.

Many buildings of importance, all designed in
good taste, grew up in Cambridge during this century.

The library of Samuel Pepys, including the manuscript of his celebrated *Diary*, was left to his old
College of Magdalene in 1703, and reached Cambridge
in 1725, when it was placed in what are now called
the Fellows' buildings, a range built to do honour
to the bequest. To the University Library, enriched
by King George I's present of Bishop Moore's collection, was added a new wing designed in the
Classical style. The Senate House as we now see it
is an eighteenth-century building, and a fine example
of its period. At King's College the Fellows' building by Gibbs is another notable addition to the architecture of the place, and the alterations at Clare,
Trinity Hall, and Emmanuel are all good of their
kind.

The beauty of Cambridge does not consist in broad
streets or in imposing public buildings. The greater
Colleges lie with their gatehouses towards the town,
their courts and lawns stretching towards the river,
which is spanned by their private bridges. Beyond
the river the eye is charmed with a vista of tall trees
and flowery gardens. In every College there lurk
particular treasures. Corpus Christi, with its old Court
abutting on the Saxon Church of St. Benet, where in
bygone days the scholars were wont to worship, can
show the hall in which Kit Marlowe dined and Parker presided. This College has one of the most in-

teresting libraries in the University, and one of the best collections of plate in the country. Jesus College has an unique chapel. Norman and Early English masonry, fine old stalls, and a mediæval organ may here be seen, and, for those who care for such things, there are windows by Morris and Burne-Jones. Examples of Wren's work in Cambridge have already been noticed. The bridge built from his designs at St. John's is illustrated in the present volume. No one should miss all there is to see in this stately College. The Combination Room is a typical Tudor gallery; and on Feast Nights, when illuminated with wax candles in silver sconces, it presents a picture unforgetably beautiful. Trinity and St. John's are the only Colleges possessed of statuary. In the anti-chapel of the former College the statues of Newton, Bacon, Barrow, Macaulay, Whewell, and Tennyson form a striking group. That of Newton is by Roubiliac, and some busts by this admirable master may be seen in the College library, where too is the celebrated statue of Byron by Thorwaldsen, and numerous enrichments of the bookcases by the hand of Grinling Gibbons. This library, which is one of the principal Collegiate libraries in Europe, has over 100,000 volumes. Among its manuscripts are the celebrated Canterbury Psalter, a volume of Milton manuscripts (including the first sketch of *Paradise Lost*), the manuscript of

Tennyson's *In Memoriam*, that of Thackeray's *Esmond*, and several Byron manuscripts. The library of St. John's College is second only to that at Trinity. It is approached by a staircase of singular beauty. At Magdalene is the Pepys Library; and the libraries of Peterhouse, Trinity Hall, and Queens' are good specimens of mediæval college collections. The University has two public libraries. Of these the University Library proper enjoys the right to a copy of every book printed in the realm. It numbers some 500,000 volumes, and is rich in every kind of literature. The rule which allows M.A.'s and certain B.A.'s to borrow books, and which gives readers access to the shelves, makes this library, as Lord Acton said, "the only useful library in Europe". The library of the Fitzwilliam Museum includes a remarkable collection of musical manuscripts, the most valuable of which are manuscripts of Bach, Handel, and Beethoven.

During the last hundred years Cambridge has been enriched with numerous laboratories and several collegiate institutions. Of the latter the most important is Downing College, built in 1805. Two professors have their maintenance here: one of Medicine, the other of the Laws of England. On Downing property the present Law Schools, Geological Museum, and other of the more recent habitations of science have been built. The great Cavendish Laboratory, to which the

seventh Duke of Devonshire was a conspicuous benefactor, was built in 1874. Almost every branch of
science now possesses its special museum, while
art and the study of antiquities are served by the
Fitzwilliam and the Archæological Museums.

Cambridge to-day is a large and complex community: the undergraduate population alone has
reached nearly four thousand souls. The Senate, or
body of M.A.'s having voting powers in the government of the University, numbers over seven thousand
persons; while the total number of members of the
University who still keep their names "on the boards"
stands at 14,758. Every kind of study, from astral
chemistry to engineering, finds among this mass of
people some professed teachers and eager students.

All this has not been a matter of natural growth.
The nineteenth century saw far-reaching changes im-
posed upon the University; though for some time,
most Fellows of Colleges were still required to take
Orders, and the rule of celibacy was enforced. By
the removal of these restrictions and by the abolition
of Religious Tests, the University has reaped much
benefit. But it has not been all gain. The amenities
of College life in many of the smaller societies have
been considerably interfered with, and that "corporate
sense" which has hitherto been the strength of the
college system has been weakened. On the other

hand, the additions which have been made to the recognized fields of intellectual activity have indisputably made for the utility of Cambridge as a centre of education; though it is possible that the demand for young teachers, both public and private, by drawing men away from private study, may tend to lessen the value of the University as a contemplative body. Of this danger not everyone seems unconscious.

As the seventeenth century was the age of Bacon, and the eighteenth century that of Newton, so the nineteenth century has been called the age of Darwin. Thus has Cambridge sent three of her sons to revolutionize the study of Natural Philosophy. Among Cambridge scientists of modern times are Adams, Airy, Herschell, Clarke-Maxwell, Stokes, Lords Kelvin, Rayleigh, Avebury, Sir James Dewar, and Sir Joseph Thompson. Cambridge as a school of medicine has been celebrated ever since the time of Caius. Its importance at the present moment is largely owing to the life and labour of the late Sir Michael Foster. Numerous Cambridge men have held professorships at Oxford during the century. The names of Maine, Sir F. Pollock, and Mr. Sidgwick at once occur to the mind; and to-day the chairs of Astronomy, Physics, Botany, Classical Archæology, and English Literature in that University are occupied by Cambridge men. From Cambridge, too, come the

CLARE COLLEGE FROM THE BACKS

Astronomer Royal, his immediate predecessor, and most of the provincial and colonial astronomers.

Popular fallacies die hard. But it is indeed remarkable that Cambridge should be supposed to give herself over to mathematical studies, when it is remembered that she produced in Bentley and Porson the two greatest classics that England ever knew; while in the nineteenth century Munro, Jebb, and Headlam have won European reputations as classical scholars; and, of the older Universities, Cambridge alone confers a purely classical degree. The Cambridge School of Theology is associated with the names of Westcott, Lightfoot, and Hort.

Modern Cambridge has been prolific in men of letters: Byron, Macaulay, Thackeray, Kinglake, Tennyson, Fitzgerald, Grote, Kingsley, Seely, F. D. Maurice, Samuel Butler, Leslie Stephen, and Maitland are names taken at random. The list of her public men is a long one and includes the great Whig peers from Palmerston, Melbourne, Grey, and Lansdowne to such men as the late Duke of Devonshire and the late Earl Spencer: the senior branch of the House of Cecil has been uniformly faithful to Cambridge since the days of the great Lord Burleigh. The Manners family have been as stoutly Cambridge; and the late Duke of Rutland, better known as Lord John Manners, was a familiar figure in the University. It is

a Cambridge College that can claim at this moment
the Speaker, the Lord Chief Justice, the Leader of
the House of Lords, the Leader of the Opposition in
the Commons, the Viceroy of India, the Ex-Viceroy,
and the retiring Governor-General of Canada.

Cambridge as a home of legal studies has been
famous since the sixteenth century: Lyndhurst, Cran-
worth, Pollock, Fitzjames Stephen are legal lumi-
naries of modern times.   Trinity Hall is the College
with which the study of law is particularly associated.
For two hundred years this College practically con-
trolled the Court of Arches, which until the nineteenth
century was some way advanced took cognizance of
all Probate and Admiralty cases, as well as of causes
arising out of ecclesiastical jurisdictions.   For some
time the Masters and Fellows appointed the Dean
of Arches, and the Master enjoyed a right to rooms
in Doctors' Commons.   Among learned Civilians who
have presided over the destinies of "the Hall" are
Sir James Exton, Sir Nathaniel Lloyd, Sir Edward
Simpson, and Sir William Wynne.   The last of this
order (for the Court of Arches lost its civil jurisdiction at this time) was Sir Herbert Jenner Fust,
whose name will long be remembered in connec-
tion with the celebrated Gorham judgment.   Sir
Herbert was succeeded in the Mastership by the
late Sir Henry Summer Maine, of Pembroke Col-

lege, sometime Corpus Professor of Jurisprudence at Oxford.

The reputation of a College for this or that study is, however, less precious to its more thoughtful inmates than are those associations with famous men long since dead which cling to every grove and every court in Cambridge: to Byron's pool at Grantchester; to Milton's mulberry tree in the Fellows' garden at Christ's; to the little tower at Queens' in which Erasmus studied; to the rooms occupied by Gray at Pembroke; to Newton's at Trinity; or to Wordsworth's at St. John's. Sometimes such traditions are well founded; but if they be not, what matter? The strength and value of such things lie in their power to cause even the youngest of us to see humanity as a grave pageant, of which we may be witnesses though only for a space. But membership of an English University carries with it experiences more personal and more intimate than these. A man may deem himself to be bestowing scant notice upon his surroundings, and yet there are a hundred impressions made upon him by sights and sounds, in these his student days, which pass patternwise into the fabric of his nature. Other phases of College life are remembered in more detail: hours passed in anxious study for the schools; boisterous gatherings when, with old wine in young bellies, almost anything seemed worth the saying; eager struggles in the field or upon the river, when the glory of the College really did seem to depend upon the muscles of some eight or fifteen carefully-dieted young men. One recalls these states of mind as facts; but they have no corresponding values in the world of sense. The really haunting memories are those of particular firesides; of the outlook from this or that window seat; of a moonlit court in summer-time, of the scent of flowers there and of the babble of the fountain; of choir music by taper light in winter; and of the ordered chimes leisurely perpetuating their Tudor cadences. Such thoughts, such recollections

"The past bestows on us,
Like showers along the dusty roads of life,
Or welcome sunbeams on some bleak grey morn,
Cheering the soul in her long pilgrimage".